# By Madeline DeFrees

# WHEN SKY
# LETS GO

# THE BRAZILLER SERIES OF POETRY
*Richard Howard, General Editor*

# WHEN SKY
# LETS GO

*Poems by*

# Madeline DeFrees

*with a note by Richard Howard*

## GEORGE BRAZILLER

*New York*

Copyright © 1978 by Madeline DeFrees
Published simultaneously in Canada by
McGraw-Hill Ryerson Limited
All rights reserved
For information address the publisher:
George Braziller, Inc.
One Park Avenue, New York 10016

Library of Congress Cataloging in Publication Data

DeFrees, Madeline.
   When sky lets go.
   (The Braziller series of poetry)
   I. Title.
PS3554.E4W5 1977     811'.5'4     76-55838
ISBN 0-8076-0844-0
ISBN 0-8076-0845-9 pbk.


First Printing
Printed in the United States of America
Designed by Kathleen Carey

*For Bernie*

# Acknowledgments

"Driving Home," *The Nation* (October 22, 1974)

"This Is How the Bridge Goes Down," *Ploughshares* (1974)

"Beach Cliff Graffiti," *Fragments* (1975)

"Nude Under the Eaves," *Woman of the Future* (forthcoming) and *Fragments* (1976)

"Indian Autobiographies," *Jeopardy* (Spring 1972)

"Winter Scene with Frozen Photographer," *Northwest Review* (Autumn 1970)

"Long Distance Call," *Occident* (Fall 1971)

"The Shell," *Cutbank 4* (1975)

"Paying My Taxes," *Poetry Northwest* (Autumn 1969)

"A Woman Possessed," *Northwest Review* (Spring 1975)

"The Odd Woman," *Choice 10*

"Watch for Fallen Rock," *Garfield Lake Review* (May 1973)

"Nights of flint and snow," *Cutbank 4* (1975)

" 'My Dream of Pure Invention,' " *The Nation* (November 19, 1973)

"Cover," "How the Amish Women Went Down in the Iowa River," *Poetry Northwest* (Summer 1976)

"Orthopedic," *Book Week* (October 30, 1966)

"Mexican Crucifix," *Sewanee Review* (Spring 1966)

"Still Life with Lumbosacral Support," *Poetry Northwest* (Winter 1972–1973)

"Filling in the Report," *Southern Poetry Review* (Spring 1974)

"Five Finger Drill for a Dry Time," *Jeopardy* (April 1969)

"Barometer," *New Republic* (September 14, 1968 and February 8, 1969)

"Baroque Lament," *Minnesota Review* (August–October 1965)

"The Breakthrough," *Poetry Northwest* (Spring 1965)

"Everything Starts with the Fall," *Poetry Northwest* (Autumn 1965)

"Pendant Watch," *Malahat Review* (July 1969)

"Frieze for a Top-Heavy Apartment," *Jeopardy* (Spring 1972)

"The Lode," *The Nation* (September 1, 1969)

"Letter to an Absent Son," *New American Review* (August 1968)

"Notes from the Top Story," *Poetry Northwest* (Autumn 1968)

"In the Hellgate Wind," *Sojourner Magazine* (1974)

"Psalm for a New Nun," *Choice 5* (1967)

"At Xavier Hall with Residents from the State School for the Handicapped," *Sewanee Review* (Spring 1975)

"Reply to an Irremovable Pastor Twenty Years Too Late," *Northwest Review* (Fall 1972)

"With a Bottle of Blue Nun to All My Friends," *American Review* (September 1973)

"Domesticating Two Landscapes," *New Republic* (September 27, 1969)

"Existing Light," *Sewanee Review* (Summer 1969)

"Night Driving," *The Garret* (1969) and *Mill Mountain Review* (1975)

"The Family Group," *Northwest Review* (Spring 1975)

"When the River Rises," *Poetry Northwest* (Autumn 1969)

"Attachments," *Poetry Northwest* (Autumn 1969)

"The Forgiveness," *Jeopardy* (Spring 1975)

"An Elegy for God and the Widow Damascus," *New American Review* (September 1967)

"The Ninth Wave," *Sewanee Review* (Spring 1975)

"Moving in Time," *The Nation* (February 16, 1974)

"Self-service Island: an Elegy from Landsend," *Chariton Review* (Spring 1975)

"The Patched Eye," *Rendezvous* (Spring 1977)

"Hope Diamonds," *American Review* (February 1973)


Certain of the poems have also appeared in the following anthologies:

"Everything Starts with the Fall," originally titled "A Catch of Summer," IV, Borestone Mountain Poetry Awards 1966, *Best Poems of 1965*. Palo Alto: Pacific Books, 1965. (Under *Sister Mary Gilbert*)

"Peninsular," Reed College Anthology for Northwest Manuscript Conference (April 1966), ed. and written out by Lloyd J. Reynolds.

"Letter to an Absent Son" and "Pendant Watch," *No More Masks! An Anthology of Poems by Women*, ed. Florence Howe and Ellen Bass. Garden City, New York: Doubleday, 1973.

"Letter to an Absent Son" and "The Wake," *Rising Tides*: 20th Century American Women Poets, ed. Laura Chester and Sharon Barba. New York: Washington Square Press, 1973.

"Driving Home," "The Family Group," "Hope Diamonds," " 'My Dream of Pure Invention,' " "Watch for Fallen Rock," and "With a Bottle of Blue Nun to All My Friends," *Modern Poetry of Western America*, ed. Clinton F. Larson and William Stafford. Provo, Utah: Brigham Young University Press, 1975.

"Existing Light" and "Indian Autobiographies," *Poets West*, ed. Lawrence P. Spingarn. Van Nuys, California: Perivale Press, 1975.

# Contents

A Note on Madeline DeFrees

## WATCH FOR FALLEN ROCK

## THE BLUE NUN

## PICTURES ON THE SHIFTING WALL

# MADELINE DEFREES

## "Day Rolls Over Me And Still It Wears Somebody Else's Sign"

In one of her letters, Louise Bogan speaks of the poetry of Sister Mary Gilbert, published in 1964: "She sees things rather panoramically, and is not at all pietistic—hardly any Jesus and NO Holy Mother. Unusual." It is one more reason to wish that Louise Bogan were alive still, this new book of poems by the woman who was once, in religion, Sister Mary Gilbert but who writes now from, and into, another life. How much *more* unusual than the diligently administered, serviceable poems of *From the Darkroom* are the extreme and charged ones of Madeline DeFrees —and how I should like to know what Bogan would have made of them, and of the fact that the same woman made them, as I say, for and from another life. What I make of them is mainly a wonderment, marveling as I do at the authority and, still, the solicitude: the authority which comes from the solicitude of their making, and the violence which works out of them, from the center to the surface, discharged there in the only enduring function, the only *effectiveness* violence can have, accommodated by art.

Not that Madeline DeFrees is immensely or immediately concerned to show us her art—but she has enough of it, she has sufficient *style*, we may call it, to control the human violence of the talent, to turn it to account. I think that in her other life, what she has, and what she does, would be called prayer, though in the life exhibited, in the life exposed here, one is not so easy about the precision of the paranoia ("One star is out to get me" . . . "Nothing here / the wind can use against me") as to be able so to call it. Until we remember Blake's beautiful definition, and we are a little easier about the metamorphosis of this poetry into prayer—unmixed attention, Blake says, is prayer.

These are poems of terrible weather, chronic vicissitudes of climate and season which will not permit us to rest in them, nor the poet to repose until she has wrestled with them and rid herself of them:

> Sisters,
> The Blue Nun has eloped with one
> of the Christian Brothers. They are living
> in a B&B Motel just out of
> Sacramento . . .
>
> ("With a Bottle of Blue Nun to
> All My Friends")

The "other people" in the poems seem maddened, driven beside themselves by some awful contention of the landscape and the lost or lawless meteorology (what Newman, if I may have my little joke with this poet of an abjured theology, called some dark aboriginal catastrophe); yet all the others—the "irremovable pastor 20 years too late," the widow Damascus, that other widow whose parrot calls her Mama, the residents from the State school for the handicapped, the rest: for there is a gathering personnel in these poems, and if they are paranoid, it is a paranoia of work done with others, pleasures shared and mourned with others, the paranoia we call, in our saner moments, life itself—are versions, try-outs, experimental takes of Madeline DeFrees, whose rages always turn upon, or against, herself and whose verses always enjamb to reveal something unexpected:

> . . . The old and strange collect around me,
> names I refuse pitched at my head
> like haloes. This one is a dead ringer.
> It rings dead. I pat the head of the beagle
> nosing in my crotch and try to appear
> grateful. A witch
> would mount the nearest broom

and leave by the chimney. At ten I plot
my exit: gradual shift to the left,
a lunge toward the bourbon . .
                    ("The Odd Woman")

a turn indeed. When we say our experience has given us a turn,
we are speaking, or might be, of such an art as that of this de-
ciduous woman, casting off the very selves—

. . . Weeks trickled off. Rouge drained
from wimpled cheeks. Warm air came back. It caught
us on the swollen porch, limp coifs
and windy veils, throwing out the garbage.
                    ("Reply to an Irremovable Pastor")

—which once had chastened her into habitual service: casting
off the habit. It is difficult not to speak personally in this matter,
in this spirit; what after all can be less exceptionable than to speak
personally when you are speaking about a *persona?* about a
woman who has made herself intimate with us without making
herself less private, public without making herself known? It is
difficult not to acknowledge and even affirm that here is the
poetry—a cause for wonder—of a woman who has spent and
gained enough of her life and her death in the one acceptation,
so much that now that she has altered the acceptation, trans-
formed the provenance, her earlier giving and taking cannot be
regarded as a parenthesis.

Better, then, to take this poetry as all the one thing, sutures
and splints for the one life growing together. It is not easy, as
I have suggested, but it is literally wonderful. Best to take it as
the snorkel diver learns to take the sea; the mask fits close, the
breathing must be through a tube clenched tight between the
teeth, and the movement afforded by the flippers is abrupt and
unaccustomed—we move and breathe and have our being in an
alien element, and these tools, the means of locomotion, are merely

there to keep us going. In the destructive element, Conrad said, immerse—let *us* say, revisional, in the alien element submit, and you shall see wonders, taken for signs:

> . . . I drive ahead
> Towards a dead end, a new freeway. Which?
> The labels don't match. Signs double back
> between the eyes. On two-lane roads
> I list toward open sea and salt, kill
> my plants at home with small attentions.
> Nobody's fault. Wreckage the stars relate
> in drifting light ought to form a scene.
> Even on Mars there is water. What
> does it all mean, this neighborliness of disaster?
> Barnacles stud the necklace of my bones.

It all means a sea-change into something rich and strange. It is how Miranda, middle-aged, renders the real.

RICHARD HOWARD

# WATCH FOR
# FALLEN ROCK

# DRIVING HOME

The wheels keep pulling
towards that sunny sideroad.
I pull them back, headed for Blue Creek.
Grasses getting thin, the rushes lean. Nothing here
the wind can use against me.


In the long stretch
after Cataldo takes the hill, I think about
Clarence Worth Love's annulment
till a nerve gives way.
The gradual curve unwinds
the river again. Now it is green in the placid
crook of my arm
as the paired hands of those days
I wanted to die.


By the Superior exit
the highway crew leaves markers
I do not trust. The diamond
watch for crossing game, for ice and rocks,
hangs a legend on my lights.
I do the same. One star is out to get me.


A level sound. Pastures graze the trees
around the shoulder.
On a high beam, the mare swings
her dark side to the moon.
Something turns over in the trunk
I think
one more time

of your black luggage
on the bed. I know
it may not carry me much longer.

# THIS IS HOW THE BRIDGE GOES DOWN

Steel arms tired of empty reaching, settle
into a bed older than the urge to get across.
No one pays attention. Losses are usual,
the elements tempered to subtraction. Only giant beams
know their own sinking for a tragic sun,
eye burning horizons that cover them.
Experts may detect a shrinking. Rails
rode earlier to the west, their faint refusal
buckling to catastrophe. That, too, was natural.
Engineers are human.

The great arms need a woman who needs them.
Not this cold strength, purged of impurities,
bent to perfect arcs. If she wants to drown,
why, help her! That lunge of water to the lip,
its cadence closing sleep to coffins, underlies
the horizontal. Steel shifts its hold.
The crevice widens.

Bridges on pontoons, bridges with concrete support.
The best bridge of all must rest in air—
airborne lovers in rainbow sleep. They dip
necks graceful as cranes to lower the weight
that rides them. Into the insinuating stream,
all cavities filled, features altered in green
light, heaviness washed clean away,
the body gives up its defenses. To be the bride
of water is the first dream, lapping our bones
in the mother dark, kissing us back when we escape
from a world older than water.

# BEACH CLIFF GRAFFITI

Already your name is worn on the rock—
gouge and scar—
sandstone kiss of knife against cliff,
the silica glare.
I take them into the circular track of the sea
under the picture-window stare
of brick and wood.

Sunstruck bodies litter the sand.
A windy bird
stretches the sky to its frame.
Slow gain of the sea
on land. I feel you moving in
with the singing surf.
My voice rides a heady wind
lost on the sea floor. Whose echo rings
off that lighthouse rock,
washes small life into tidepools?

I tunnel under the long roar
to that far cove where your hands gather
the moody night. Whose image?
Whose inscription? Impartial sun
looks into particular marks,
the unlettered code of climbers
the crude moon leaves in shadow. Now

I touch your sign
with earth-moving fingers
the world slides from under
the shifting slope near dune grass

my legend, line, in tune
with the salty racetrack and marine bodies,
with the maned waves.

# NUDE UNDER THE EAVES

I have learned the disposition of her limbs,
the face removed from consequence
by lazy strokes across the cloudy waters moving
towards her thighs. Little harbor lights
on breast and nipple,
the missing hand that holds them
in the still white frame.

I want the Saltspring color of her days
to come from you in this body
lifted out of its frame.
She suns her charcoal legs at the firelit wall
night deepens as the tide turns over
the pelt of winter—always winter
on the greying seaswept face.

I have earned the dispossession of her eyes
unmade, my foot drawn animal in sand,
lids lowered to avoid
the ritual bells gone foolish.
The channel tolls the weight, each vow
she might have paid. I let them out,
draw around me their missing length, paying them over

old lover's chant at the iron grate
of this November bride.

# A SIMPLE TEST

These absences known in the body are true
black wings
of theatrical birds beamed
towards the island's tallest ash.
The white flap of waves mapping the boat's
way of impressing itself is not
true. Flowers on furlough,
season of dead leaves
ploughed under by frost
real as the map on my wall: flat
and faithful.

The wine bottle green
as the Portuguese town of its label
gathers the light to represent it.
Amen. It is false.
Saw-tooth clusters of fern brought home
from the wood, wear their disease
like medals, endure like the ache in my arm.
Do not trust them. They only pretend
to be heroes. Arms wide to the plate glass
the Indian brave rides bareback
the painted brick of the fireplace.

Sad hounds in a pastel
leap from their frame,
yield to the subtle nude. Shades
of dogwood lie
over the bird feeder, true
to themselves. The home loving quail
dead under a picture the body wanted to enter.
And you, Reader, your face moved slowly

over this page like a lens
intended to magnify
it-is-not-true

# INDIAN AUTOBIOGRAPHIES

*For Gary Kimble*

I have no way of knowing how you tracked me here.
Maybe a dry branch cracked in the forest heart.
A puff of smoke twisted to begin its lazy climb.
We did not move. The night was ours. I watched a maple leaf
turn over in your face and die. Clues we dropped
along the way were just a game for tourists.
Cigar-store Indians and those cute, concentric nuns.
We wound them up and let them take the stage
and watched each other from the eyes behind our eyes.

How many cigarettes to bring me peace?
You let me wander the ground over and over
When you knew every pore in the moss,
the shadow a bird makes, the river of dew
in a leaf's concave, you said
some terrible gentle word that sent me back
to the place it all began. We learned
to keep still in dialects so old our trust
restored the language. Collectors dug up scraps
of dirty blankets, framed them, amazed
at their design. Where sun can't penetrate
there may be time to use cold shade for cover,
prove the race is human.

                    Late fall again outside.
Half-breeds remember. We tie a scarlet rag
on the tamarack and sink our lightweight steps
in the looked-for snow.

# THE WAKE

I am sitting on your Indian rock watching the third
light go out, larger, in the ditch farther down.
When all those stricken wind chimes catch
a snagtooth pine I am with you, pitched
like a tuning fork to your stark room
on Hyde Street in the City of the Golden Gate.

I wanted to crash the gate. Steady the night
that beat your threatened ground. A clutch
to disengage old drives: that head under the wheel
of the ocean road, turned helmet-white on the shoulder.
Asleep in a violent land, huge gears unlock.
The right sounds mesh, hand easy on the choke.

A shift into all weathers. We talk of going out
to the engine's relaxed running. The naked stand
on the soggy bath mat, everything slipping away
like a shoreline. Or into manic wind, our dead-end
words blown back into our faces. If people say,
"When she washed dishes like surf on Acapulco . . . "

we'll lean into that legend, weathered beams shifting,
everything moving out past the breakwater. The older drift
of single lives, true as rock to lichen. Covered by more
than the lover's body, we let the pared moon haul us in,
ride the hovercraft that barely touches water. Sky falls
into the sea. The dark wings past the window widen.

# WINTER SCENE
## WITH FROZEN PHOTOGRAPHER

The man I love is blacker than this blizzard,
his shoulder to the storm on fast film over forty.
A streetlamp burned this bush. The twig was willow.
No use to rub him out. The park's deserted.
All guns were loaded.

If snow goes on forever is the tube exhausted?
The film across my eyes says tearful valley.
It could be warm, late anger or a gift-wrapped
wedding. The rice I carry home to cook
until December.

The lost repeat the lost at intersections.
Square frosted bulbs spin flies in dying
blizzards. I cross my fingers on a ring,
confetti sucked into the lungs from fat stacks
shocked to hear it.

The image matters on the page. Mirage and ghosts
won't stop it: a storm of headlights driving like the devil.
The man I love lies easy as a blizzard.
I cross my heart to take him in. And room
is all I have.

# LONG DISTANCE CALL

*For Warren*

I see you standing in a closed space in that
cold country
counting your coins, knowing
what both of us have left: some vision
of the ultimate wreck, bodies
dragged to the slag-heap.
When a lead pipe taps frosted glass
I look up with you at the black face
filling your window past the broken connection.
I feel afraid enough for two
seeing you pick up the change. You are safer now
held in the middle distance.

I stole from you often, proud that you knew three
languages, all of them violent.
One, I could understand. In a race of suicides,
widowed queens, gambling towns,
I reviewed your lines, watching you burn
your Presbyterian father's ghost in dry ice.
Two times I made a weak accomplice
to your anger.

Now if I turn my cheek
towards New Jersey and that dim street, it is
for the blow we both saw coming: a hit-and-run kiss
to teach our tears cold storage.

# THE SHELL

My sealed house winters in its triple shell—
storm-windowed, weather-
stripped and double-locked. I knock
icicles from the low eaves and watch the cold
come back cold
air condensing under doors. Sculptured carpet
snow below the cocomat. Once
I wanted that
blood too thick and hot
for comfort, all breath closer
than my own. Ice
forms again on the lintel, hardens
against the screen.

                In your light
sleep I pull back the drapes,
let the cold
light down, leave the flue open. Animal signs
of a long siege. Later
the barometer falls. Wind
hollows a track through the chimney. Casings
crack as they swell. The house
settles into the frozen ground.

# PAYING MY TAXES

The Internal Revenue agent visits me only
by night. We are old friends, newly acquainted.
I tell him I do not have to pay. He talks
in decibels of Leavenworth. He knows
what I am worth before he goes away.
"You need someone to take care
of you. Someone down here."
Prophecy or mistake, a cold computer
let me take that paper man, my lone exemption.
I love him as I may to widen
the walls of my prison, make the government pay.
Tough as he is, he faces up to forms.
I keep them in a desk drawer with a safety
catch. Computer love is like the poetry:
more exciting when routines break down.
Nevada's never been my kind of state.
But in the evergreens of Washington
we shoot for the moon
and learn to gamble on the government.

# A WOMAN POSSESSED

*her face blasted like a medieval weeper*
GARCIA LORCA

She remembered the charge.
A day like any other fall.
Her red shirt taunted dark shapes
in the street. The loud report
when that half-smile,
turned loose to goad the gusty animal,
stepped out to meet what waited.
She wanted to cast her body on the horns
of that forgetful season.
Black sounds hurtled from the chute.
The crowd looked on.

In that arena, narrowed to a skull
bone china shivered.
Clatter of Spode and Wedgwood
on mosaic tile.
The cameo relief of eyes glazed forward,
a crater where the trapped shale
burst its cone. Lava flowed
from thick veins into rock and there was more besides
the charred unknown
thin plates cracked
the sealed jar

on the grandstand shelf.
It may be, her reflexive feint
rushed the first dark lover,
proud blood in knotted streams. All night
the mad roar swelled

rain on the slack-limbed trees. Wet faces massed
on pavement. Nothing but this late fall.
It rumbled down on simple characters: a man
a legendary mount
a bull. Clay of their common drama
and the woman, old.

# THE ODD WOMAN

At parties I want to get even,
my pocket calculator rounds everything off,
taught to remember. I'm not so good
at numbers, feel awkward
as an upper plate without a partner.
Matched pairs float from the drawing board
into the drawing room, ears touched
with the right scent,
teeth and mouth perfect.

The cougar jaw yawns on the sofa back,
his molars an art-object.
The old and strange collect around me,
names I refuse pitched at my head
like haloes. This one is a dead-ringer.
It rings dead. I pat the head of the beagle
nosing in my crotch and try to appear
grateful. A witch
would mount the nearest broom

and leave by the chimney. At ten I plot
my exit: gradual shift to the left,
a lunge toward the bourbon. The expert hunters
are gutting a deer
for the guest of honor. Soft eyes
accuse my headlights. I mention early
morning rituals. A colleague
offers to show me the door I've watched
for the last hour.

We come to my coat laid out
in the master bedroom, warm hands curled

in the pocket. I know
how a woman who leaves her purse behind
wants to be seduced. I hang mine
from the shoulder I cry on.
Say goodnight to the Burmese buddha,
hunters in the snow,
and leave for the long river drive to town.

# WATCH FOR FALLEN ROCK

Seeing the coyote flash across the road,
outcrop of stone, the fawn
shy among reluctant green, I can entertain
the Amazon virgin on the ship's prow
bearing down. Remember how, wave after wave,
the overwhelming line from hip to ankle
determined that foreshortened
figure. Unlike the bronze pope destroyed
she never stayed where air was too thin
for the sea's germane reflections.

Her wooden image sent me back to gather rock
roses in the canyon. Porcelain petals
flared like bone.
A herd of grasses rippled over the cliff.
Where winter had opposed
black ice in all the passes
it was as if those toppled urns
outside our coastal window
let the sea disguise what sun could not
set fire to.

In surprising turns the road signs missed,
ghosts of antelope and elk
might glow an instant in our headlights
and go under
while at home we watched
the deer and frost move in
to claim our bronze chrysanthemums.

fill with your long absence, the wind
not bitter,
ice, an age to come. When sky lets go
it is warm work digging you out,
headlight cold in the socket,
one branch of the cedar
down.

      The compost path
steepens on both sides of the summer-
house. I think of old mines
reopened: veins of chard,
sad pods in coal-dark seams, the golden load
unfolding in the buried ear. I ride the waves,
green, to the sea
warm rain.

          Weathered beets. The seal-faced kelp
torn from its rank salt bed
and the puckered kiss
of anemone.

         Water turns us back,
road and river curving under ice
to the deepening source. Home. Inside
your place is warm
plum and apple slowly turning wine.

## "MY DREAM OF PURE INVENTION"

Nothing comes to a halt sleeping off
the highway. There is snow
on the ground in Harrisburg. Icicles hang
from eaves
the tired scenes unreel. Night comes
into its own
sidewalk cafes. The white safaris
open wings
in the Oriental Pyrenees. We seed the clouds
waiting for our lives
to fall on us. The marriage in Mexico a rumor
all that summer.

Around a potbellied stove
our hands warm
we check the positions of stars
pinned against the storm windows,
double back
towards Plum Creek where cattle drowse
in their snowy stalls.
All roads closed.

Remember winter in Berlin, the places we have been
together.
The bamboo forest
darkness whistles through,
travel folder lies
opened like accordions. The moon, too,
that first disturber of sleep.
This broken day an early sun recalls
the hands, everything cheap when we pretend
pulling away from the body.

# COVER

I went along on the map to Virginia,
said your name like the rape
of women who should have run for cover
to the Iowa river,
those days of ease and clover
never carried home.

Wet through I stand under the folding
umbrella of your concern, the clouds
uncertain as that first day
you fell on me and I learned
where our roots were tending. A knot of wind
dissolves. You forget how I grow

away from you all these weeks,
my one good eye turned honest for the asking.
I bend over radical leeks to follow
revelations of the sun
when petals flare,
their sudden stamina.

Whatever blade's on fire by the gate, going
to seed, going wise to sleep, we fill
the exiled body, animal caves, feeling them
open. The heavens
fall on thin skin. Outside.
This mortgaged apple
paradise.

# HOW THE AMISH WOMEN
## WENT DOWN
## IN THE IOWA RIVER

Went down under quilted leaves,
the beards of their men
rough against homespun cloth.
Went down on the green verge without a sigh
under broad-brimmed hats,
the logjammed stream of their coming
overriding the shore. The hostler unhitched
and watered the horses.
Girls in their Sunday dark, white caps and aprons,
sheered the fragrant night.

Down like a jet from Moline at 30,000 feet
with the throttle open
in the shade of horsedrawn carts,
sad boots on cobbled streets of a country town.
Went down in the heat
of iron kettles filled
with boiling lard. Elders in black felt hats
shook their heads and warned.
The tactful fathers spared, let down
their guard and turned away.

Now it is noon when the women rise.
Their cottonwood stand of simmering trees lapped
in light. Bonnets down to the groin,
they are caught in the April freeze
of the floodplain. The river grips them hard,
full loins skewed
to the mouth of summer

# THE BLUE NUN

# PENINSULAR

My own voice brings you back
over the dark night waves
wide as the sea's arms and the wind's
enclosure, lapping the disparate shores
with a somber echo or breaking on bone-
white sand with a thundering nearness.

Your face moves under the fractured
waters, always and never the same
in the deep green light. And the cry
of wheeling seasons lengthens across
your shadow, lost in the wavering image
my eyes refract.

     Child or grandfather
god in the seaweed silence, wrapped
in the streaming bands or the bearded surge:
I drown you in each new day, but the body
rises to float, face down,
on the crest of a quartered moon.

I cannot call over the roiling tide;
my ears drum with a hollow, dumb containment,
and my voice comes back, back, like a message
in a bottle, sealed in the universal vessel,
home to the harbor's continental drift
to break its narrow neck on the structured rock.

# ORTHOPEDIC

Many times in dreams I awake
in a hospital bed, my foot or hand
remote on a plaster cross overhead,
suspended beyond my control
where extremities join in rivets of pain.

A wave from the sterile brain goes out:
O lost among women, reclaim
your inheritance of nerve and bone,
rein in your disobedient members and observe
today's fast for tomorrow's famine.
Where you have been will carry you.

All the world appears ambidextrous.
Slight of hand and fleet of foot
acrobats and dancers move to music,
pirouette on a dime, or hand-over-hand
mount ropes to the improbable top
while I clump, heavy-handed, on club feet,
a lump of deactivated matter,
or black blob on a stick.

                    Nevertheless, if the amoeba
from one cell can make two
this low life, with a little luck, may renew
these alien extensions cemented
and strung up there; grace lighten
these limbs that languish like spare parts
and fuse them with my salvaged self
beyond the wrench and crush of each day's
anguish on my high white shelf.

# MEXICAN CRUCIFIX

The body is its own cross.
Woven of silver wire
a brier crown angled
like a sombrero covers
the half-moon face.

Around the loins a band
of silver slants toward
the bent knees, relaxed
and reverent together, as if
suffering were more than a posture.

A drop of sweat from the hot
metal, anchors the spine
before it disappears behind
the cloth to divide till both
feet are joined by a nail.

Upright or prone, the figure
retains its simple lines
on the red-brown wood
with three rivets for support
and chained to the dark decades.

# STILL LIFE WITH
## LUMBOSACRAL SUPPORT

My monkeybar and traction geared me for this stretch.
If I could write *Corsage with Corset*
in a hand that didn't shake,
raise the body in these words, and, growing wild
unearth a shock of fireweed,
I could take the simple cure prescribed, endure
the nervous system. This wide-mouthed
tumbler from a better year
spills thistles on my black décor.
I know that proud spine. Pain
moves it. Extends the possible, slow exercise
that brings me to my knees. I believe

things I drop will be picked up on time.
Hairpin turns, knitting
needles, the lumbar strain receding.
Between steel tracks a complex
cord articulates dependence. I come to terms.
Sisters of Charity welcome me home.
Their bills have backbone. I call my friendly
witchdoctor to counteract
the breakdown. Trussed for the difficult routine
I limp to bed, a laggard
disc of moon
abject sensations, high on codeine and coffee.

Night contracts its thin
reflexive arc. The switchboard signals
every shade of risk. I step out,
cautious, into total dark.

# FILLING IN THE REPORT

Those weeks I took turns
being that accident prone woman in strange beds
settled at last by the mirror.
The corduroy spread
keyed to its bright partner keeps me awake
in the dark, one fixed pupil
letting in too much red.
Light flushes an unsound elbow,
traces the slight spinal curvature. Moves to explore
the murmuring heart tripped
by old favors.
Fingers probe a deviant ear,
follow the scar
stitching the void to my head.

At night stretched softer than pine
I look for a plot that really fits, some ground
of final ease. Nothing corresponds.
Blood in my wrist
divides against the temple.
Propped by artificial heat I turn over
your advice
practise being left-handed.
Simply to end by will this dominance of the right.
Read me another verdict—black
to match my prediction.

Farther west crows have taken over the live green
twelve gargoyle heads
turned in a uniform direction I know.
What their silence means
will never move as the world revolves. Small cries

cut to nothing
I fall asleep at the edge of winter
its thin blade at my throat.

# FIVE FINGER DRILL
## FOR A DRY TIME

My ears argue with a jackhammer
that all summer long were riddled with rain:
blown torrents reaching down to that place
where nothing has ever touched bottom
and everything is falling, falling still.

Somewhere in that abandoned well
doves quarrel with their white reflection
poised perfect on the dark lip
of a lake of sludge. My hands are busy
with routines, tension exactly right,
rhythms too slight to trip a pulse
but moving toward the grand design crafted
from cud-chewing sheep stupid before the shearing
or the wild mountain goat brought low.

Knit, purl, the needless clack. Mechanical,
my fingers ache in sockets of my skull—
crevasses too steep or sharp for wind or sleep
to lodge in—shape the round moments into a shift
to keep out cold or muffle the war with noise.

My eyes caught up in the warp, watch
the hammer's senseless drumming on the dead surface
of my brain: longer than the drop is deep,
time drills more raucous than the rain
that cries against my roof and blends
with ocean winds and tears as reticent
as icicles. Till, numb- and nimble-fingered, I break
them off to knit the strands of alien
sounds with my own stormy breathing.

# BAROMETER

Over the wreck of winter another season
crashes on this unprotected coast, cryptic
with April flotsam and the dried lavender tears
of wisteria. All through a cold spring
it has been snowing somewhere at the back
of my mind. Sleet covers a hulk dredged
from weeds to bleach on salt islands. Ashore,
ivy quickens on brick faces; over
the seawall forsythia in sunlight
flares, and cherry in white mounds chastens
the drowning eye.

                Hollow with the tug and slap
of far tides in a strict cove, I swallow
the whole ocean at one look
and in the shadow of the rock, breathe
in the drift of the sand.

## POOR PEOPLE'S PROPHET:
## A WOODPRINT

*"an axe for the frozen sea within . . ."*

All week I've tried to glass the eyes, my dead
hand, white on white, reviewing negative
shapes. Whatever chance light fades
I keep that black face by my bed,
pry into my darkness through those wooden
sockets. And where the interrupted forehead
crowds its frame, I know the pennies on my lids,
my tin resentments. To put my fingers where
the bullet hit, disclose its route, remember
what was said on camera, I cut through the wood
for clues. Here is a balcony scene, suggested
in the grain, old as the first reeling love:
two bodies estranged in the thin film
of our breathing.

           Dark birds at my window, your beaks
hooked on a song, I know what fills my room.
Its head rolls from my blade, falls from my bare
hands, explodes in the gunsight wound.
I skirt the eyes of my brother. Another trophy
hangs. Slowly the wood distends, the shroud unwinds.
Three nails relent. Along the forgotten ache
of my breath coming back, a nerve twitches.

# BAROQUE LAMENT

Thistle. The name bleeds on the tongue
and the sessile leaves deny the curious
a handhold. These weeds are nature's mourning
for the unreclaimed. They flower profanely
on delivered ground and lift their passion
into regal attitudes.

Crowned with this wounding flare, the common lot
looks singular: light flows from secular stone
into a structure bleak as bone, and water dawns
over the dark root, to ignite the silken center
in the spiny shoot.

"Keep back!" the ranged barbarities decree
through kingdoms of the damned, crying unequal loss.
"What do you know of this crooked symmetry—
knowledge and love on the antique cross—
whose fingers dulled in canvas would intrude
upon the flower of my solitude?"

# THE BREAKTHROUGH

And the skunk came, singular (I hoped)
though the stink was loud as a multitude,
pervasive as fear where I walked in the shadow
more afraid than before with the watchdog beside me
and tried to be neutral and couldn't
like Adam who wore the figleaf
and waited detection.

Away from the wood I was peaceful at first
like the rational being I am, in a Franciscan orgy
of loving my brain understood but refused to convey
to my nose. "We are both God's creatures," I said,
"whatever his stripe, and we know what it's like
when onlookers harden and sniff from a great way off."
But I knew that I had to know more.

His fur, my informant declared, from the seventeenth
floor of a building downtown, was glossy and soft;
his fluid drive, activated on attack, was chemically
sure and could be manufactured in a lab
from scientific interest or pure spite; the white
stripe was a trademark; domesticated, he could be
tailored to conform, a regular pet.

                            I agreed. And yet
I could not go to meet him in the skin, although
I saw him everywhere: in the vague rustle of bushes,
the innocent puppy rushes and the tautened ear;
in the blur of the hurtled rock, the shape at the foot
of the stair blocking escape; the wild
scattering of birds pursued
and the dreams defiled.

Today with the rain cooling our summer fevers
I stay inside with the hate and the fear,
rehearse what I think I know of the protective sac
and try to imagine the ultimate year beyond black
and white, past the stench Arabia's perfumes
cannot sweeten, and blanch at the scent
of the habit I wear, through a screen of detergent
and lotion, clean linen and prayer
or the ritual washings.

What gods can devour the distance?

I despair of the Madison Avenue mind: the dollar sign
over the lair—*THINK MINK!* And the vats full
of soap that can never be pried, by religion or law,
from the grip of a generation—mine and yours. Mine
most of all, who parade through the violent street
towards the freedom of undisguised love, not spared
the sting of the flesh I deny and am vowed
to be whiter than.

# EVERYTHING STARTS WITH THE FALL

Michaelmas rings in the air
and the rain of that fallen brightness,
petals that darken the mind
though the ground is too dry to sustain them.
"Who is like God?" and the little ones
fade into dust that denies them.
The road winds and the hills curve
outstripping the keenest glance
towards alas or he-loves-me.

It will not serve—today or any day
on the green banks of forever—
that up in the succulent garden,
tall and tended, the gold-
eyed glorious ones
bear kingly witness.

No. I will stay outside
in the doomsday weather,
the round of ruin that knows me
and brought me here. Courting
the wide lost lakes
and the wind's reverses. With the brim-
stone leaves struck down
by a sigh or a silence.

I shall go on falling in a subterranean
autumn plunge through the echoing
space with the petaled legions.
Everything falls from grace:

stars, empires, sparrows.
I move in the swordlight play
of that downward journey.

# PENDANT WATCH

In Missoula, Montana, where the townsfolk water
the sidewalks, and the Clark Fork River barely interrupts
the usual flow of traffic on Higgins Avenue, I pass,
outside a furniture store, the world's largest
captain's chair. In it sits the world's largest captain,
native to Montana, foursquare and friendly,
with a timeless eye trained on the University
while the mountain flashes holding heaven
in a mist the rest of us steer clear of.

Still agile at forty-odd, I could shinny up
that walnut leg to lie in the lap of the god,
call him husband or lover, warm as any woman in a clockwork
swoon. Except that some more concentrated fire balanced
the cogs, married gut to metal. Today's AP wire
ticks off: Nun Burns Self to Death, and in eight-point type
from Saigon, a Buddhist virgin goes out in sheer fire
while I splutter cold a spark at a time.

Time hangs golden at my breast, a decoration in disrepair
that may not run much longer. Still, I am there beside
that well-regulated throne or bed, not altogether dead.
And the captain knows. And I know. We have it timed to the
                                                    second.

# FRIEZE FOR A
## TOP-HEAVY APARTMENT

I sit alone watching your screen in borrowed light,
the cake you didn't eat filling the room,
and remember how you came over the barefoot
grass to find the place I live in. The angle
sharpens on the last flight. Red carpet,
grey. I answer every knocking radiator,
green walls my steady callers. The cluttered
evidence of half a life opened to take you in.
I gave you my misgivings: scraps of sermons, foolish
notions, love you didn't need. I learned
to be there when you called; not to grudge
your pledge to be for everyone. I wait in line
behind a bridge club, fourteen boys, a Scottie
and a ski jump. The football team, impossible
missions, priests who come to town. You taught me
the world turns, showed the way to the monk's cave,
how to be a host. On days I've lost you don't say
the kettle's black but smile and bring a Wedgwood
lamp, a silver jewel box—the odd necessities
like a guide to Italy in red leather. The Dolci
madonna approves. If only I could give you
something you need: a water buffalo, a trip
to Egypt on a cricket's wing. Somebody older
than both of us has slanted the ceiling, my muse
a friendly rock crusher, King Kong
for a valentine. I let the feeling out
in poems on paper sealed with your bond. If you find
any holes in the amices, sound the fire alarm,
wear the herringbone, hand-made
scarf I gave you at your own risk.

# THE LODE

*For Ed Lahey*

I've watched you turn your face away
a hundred times, withdrawing to the far side
of the pit my eyes alone can follow.
Wanting to be with you I mine my own
dark metal, as ignorant of terms
as any woman.

In your troubled glass where copper
glints back sunburn from your hair,
gold is a lie to keep the race alive.
You will not meet me there. You drink alone.
Huge bones block your door. Eyes of stone, unclear,
draw you underground. I cannot handle
power or machines.

I want to lift the miner's mask
that scares me less than terrors showing through.
You will not let me. I back off
wounded as your childhood town with its Irish
never-ending wake.

Years ago beside the dull Pacific
I dug my first expensive mine
with no more capital than a bright child
could borrow from aluminum sun, shafts of rain.
Days roll over me and still it wears
somebody else's sign.

Tunnels stretch from my crumbling coast
inland, far from any home. I must

45

have met you there. Young enough
to be the son I look for in the dark:
some image of a god as real as loss. Close
as steel in my side.

I've walked behind you through
a gaping town, nothing but nerve
to hold me on the edge; felt your anger
shake the few remaining houses
and recognized this six-foot
rage for love.

Machines more dangerous for being uninspected
grind towards catastrophe, their gears
held together by a common safety pin.
God is a one-eyed gambler.
Over his shoulder I watch the great lift
lower out of light and sit here staring
at these shiftless woman's hands.

# LETTER TO AN ABSENT SON

It's right to call you son. That cursing alcoholic
is the god I married early before I really knew him:
spiked to his crossbeam bed, I've lasted thirty years.
Nails are my habit now. Without them I'm afraid.

At night I spider up the wall to hide in crevices
deeper than guilt. His hot breath smokes me out.
I fall and fall into the arms I bargained for
sifting them cool as rain. A flower touch could tame me.
Bring me down that giant beam to lie submissive
in his fumbling clutch. One touch. Bad weather
moves indoors: a cyclone takes me.

How shall I find a shelter in the clouds, driven by
gods, gold breaking out of them everywhere?
Nothing is what it pretends. It gathers to a loss
of leaves and graves. Winter in the breath.
Your father looked like you, his dying proportioned
oddly to my breast. I boxed him in my plain pine
arms and let him take his ease just for a minute.

# NOTES FROM THE TOP STORY

The widow under my third floor goes for honey and henna,
coos night and morning to a pet parrot whose
language laces her name with innuendo. Intricate
his ways of gilding the *Hilda*. Survivor of a married son
and one shadowy husband, the parrot links
her half-life with whatever comes later.

Two flights up, I sit knitting to rock-
and-roll, my head swarming with dead birds who won't
talk and wouldn't be able to name me. Eager, I taste
a strange tongue, study to listen in doubles, plume
myself on having no parrot to call me Mama.
That bird grudges a step on the stair, a voice in the hall.

I hear him early and late being taught
dependence. Therefore, my step gets lighter,
lighter, as I hurry past the widow's cage,
the love-seat on the landing, and climb when I'm
tired, skip when I'm not, to my stop-
gap convent in a convertible attic.

# IN THE HELLGATE WIND

January ice drifts downriver
thirty years below the dizzy bridge. Careening traffic
past my narrow walk
tells me warm news of disaster. Sun lies
low, can't thaw my lips. I know
a hand's breadth farther down could freeze me solid
or dissolve me beyond reassembling.
Experts jostle my elbow.
They call my name.
My sleeves wear out from too much heart.

When I went back to pick up my life
the habit fit strangely. My hair escaped.
The frigidaire worked hard while I slept my night
before the cold trip home.
Roots of that passage go deeper than a razor
can reach. Dead lights
in the station end access by rail.
I could stand still to fail the danger,
freeze a slash at a time, altitude for anaesthetic.
Could follow my feet in the Hellgate wind
wherever the dance invites them.

The pure leap I cannot take stiffens downstream,
a millrace churned to murder.
The siren cries
at my wrist, flicks my throat, routine
as the river I cross over.

## PSALM FOR A NEW NUN

*My life was rescued like a bird from the fowlers' snare.*
It comes back singing tonight in my loosened hair

as I bend to the mirror in this contracted room
lit by the electric music of the comb.

With hair cropped close as a boy's, contained in a coif,
the years made me forget what I had cut off.

Now the glass cannot compass my dark halo
and the frame censors the dense life it cannot follow.

Like strength restored in the temple this sweetness wells
quietly into tissues of abandoned cells;

better by as much as it is better to be
a woman, I feel this gradual urgency

till the comb snaps, the mirror widens, and the walls recede.
With head uncovered I am no longer afraid.

*Broken is the snare and I am freed.*
*My help is in the name of the Lord who made*
*heaven and earth.* Yes, earth.

# AT XAVIER HALL WITH RESIDENTS
## FROM THE STATE SCHOOL
## FOR THE HANDICAPPED

*For Michele Birch*

We live here by touch, the dim blue light
of the nearly blind. It is right to work at the fringe,
the twilight zone, in quiet we made for ourselves.
We do not cringe at the words. The much-maligned
dark of exile keeps them new, does not bewilder
our brains. We feel small pity for the mute.
Their subtle signs flash past. Grotesque reminders
twist a mimic foot, unhinge the tongue.

At night I follow revels of the young:
parade of homeward canes, their thin batons,
thud of padded chairs, a cleft moan dredged from some
misshapen throat. Among such furniture,
my balance gone, walls thin from too much
handling, I crash and stumble. Once a slight
dark girl was rocking on her heels at the stairway foot.
My eyes began to flutter. I stubbed a purple toe.

You played the nurse that night, a pillow for my hurt,
your fingers on my forehead cool, a touch of Braille.
I used to hang my face on mirrored walls.
The flat, unflattering gaze and cracked diagonals
wrecked everything they saw. My crossed-out
eyes retreated, looked the other way.
Today we do not mind the plumbing nights, can bear
the wrench next door, ghostly voice of intercoms,

remaining calm ourselves. We've learned to live
with pain, brace of steel on flesh, crippled
vision, crazy eyes. We live at the edge
by touch, a lucky match struck against
the void beyond our tapping canes.

# REPLY TO AN IRREMOVABLE PASTOR
## TWENTY YEARS TOO LATE

Some trouble with the drains beyond repair, you said,
afraid of enlarging stains even when they came
from hell. We'd rigged your chair opposite the wall
that leaked Abe Lincoln's profile round
the bishop's goldrimmed frown. Rain, a better painter
than the local handyman, slapped our living room
with lumpy plaster every spring. Ritual
gesture meant to seal us in. No raven,
Miss Maloney manned the lookout station
in your kitchen, trained a spinster eye on backdoor
callers. She brought us angel food. Our front
gate nailed to order kept off tramps.
The sly ones climbed our fence. That German priest
who pitched his tent on woe knocked every afternoon.
His lamentations seeped into the woodwork. Light
drained from window wells. The sanitation
board wrote mildewed letters when the king
of seagulls screamed our dead-end street.
On Halloween Mother Superior held a witchy
flashlight while a novice pulled out nails.
Destructive boys, you said. Spare change would drive
them home. Weeks trickled off. Rouge drained
from wimpled cheeks. Warm air came back. It caught
us on the swollen porch, limp coifs
and windy veils, throwing out the garbage.

# WITH A BOTTLE OF BLUE NUN
## TO ALL MY FRIENDS

### 1

Sisters,
The Blue Nun has eloped with one
of the Christian Brothers. They are living
in a B&B Motel just out of
Sacramento.

### 2

The Blue Nun works the late shift
in Denver. Her pierced ears
drip rubies
like the Sixth Wound.

### 3

This is to inform you
that the Blue Nun
will become Mayor of Missoula
in the new dispensation.
At fifty-eight she threw her starched coif
into the ring and was off to a late win
over Stetson and deerstalker,
Homburg and humbug,
Church and State.

### 4

When you receive this you will know
that the Blue Nun
has blacked out
in a sleazy dive
outside San Francisco.
They remember her in Harlem.

She still carried her needle case
according to the ancient custom.


5

You may have noticed
how the walls lean towards the river
where a veil of fog hides a sky diver's
pale descent. The parachute
surrounds her like a wimple.
That's what happens when Blue Nuns
bail out.
It's that simple.

# PICTURES ON THE
# SHIFTING WALL

# DOMESTICATING TWO LANDSCAPES

Where I wait, huge sea rhythms roll. Winds
cover chimes, flow on anonymous errands
to mornings after. Forgotten toast still burning,

I try to remember who it was that went down.
One of the crew? No use. "Walk on water," he said.
If somebody answers today I'll know I was afraid.

I can't hold my head above the laundry.
Every day out there, hulls and shells and ruined bodies
wash ashore. Women lament. Comb the beach

for signs or souvenirs, foam slapping at ankles,
faces tight. For years I watched them from the ridge.
Waves held me upright. That was earlier, somewhere

I can't go back. Salt rises in my closed throat,
waves follow everywhere I run. The mountain
tells me I'll be crushed. Sea flushes

out of my ears. Bulk bears me down, rears
above the surface spitting rock. When an island saves
you from drowning it burns you out. Centuries to come

monastery bells may shimmer through sea-green silence
in lyric washes; stones melt on an unsuspecting town
hot from a friendly mountain to cast the skiing neighbors

in ceramic postures. The fluted empty cup
of a blueberry muffin, warm from the oven, stiffens
beside your plate. The cycle run, I go to join the washing

hang it all on the line. Temperature at normal,
the frigidaire hums grace. Our bones follow, but
we keep them in their chairs. After the meal

you will know that the soft word from a cold tap
or the electric range, echoes uneasy
under snow and terrified of being heard.

# EXISTING LIGHT

*For Lee Nye*

A picture is worth a thousand words
of waiting. I thought I knew and waited
with the turn. The mirrors we were not
supposed to notice, circle my bedroom walls
to help me learn. In the corner of my closet
where that other black self hangs
praying for a pumpkin coach to cart away
the ashes of a prince, something lost or
spirited below, wakes up and stretches
in the early autumn sun, to let a loose wind
trifle with the veil. Outside, the fevered leaves
repeat my fall in choruses more ancient
than my own, and underneath the stairs,
a guttural parrot calls tired
obscenities to a woman who lives alone.

I studied my unknown face in every opaque
glass, searched for the lie I kept
bottled in. Then you shot
with a focused eye to get inside
the compromising skin. Wherever the light
touched my body it left a bruise.
The bruise deepened to shadow, and shadow
flowed into shape. I felt my bones bend
against the vast concrete. Muscles
tell me what they were for in a dark
beginning of hope. Deftly you planned the angles
to cancel out reflections from my glasses.
Your strategies were natural and sure.
Light from a used sun flooded the street
where I stood, half woman, half nun, exposed.

# NIGHT DRIVING

Back through woods, past forks, roadblocks,
forgotten falls, colors that film my eyes,
steady as a child's. Tonight I will pay again
for the call that never connects. Already, rain
intones Greek, Old French, late Latin.
Words are maudlin: tears, my only tongue.
My voice, sentenced for fifty years
wants to get out. Waiting won't do.
I hear the hiss of cuttings
green with their own life. It clings
to my hair. Oxidized air comes through.
Cold in the oven mitt her smoky hand dissolves.
Half of her wide wedding band crushes my finger.
One more accident: an old-fashioned wringer,
gold driven through skin. An artist friend
puts wrenches in all his works, unwilling
to settle for curves or angles. I drive ahead
towards a dead end, a new freeway. Which?
The labels don't match. Signs double back
between the eyes. On two-lane roads
I list towards open sea and salt, kill
my plants at home with small attentions.
Nobody's fault. Wreckage the stars relate
in drifting light ought to form a scene.
Even on Mars there is water. What
does it all mean, this neighborliness of disaster?
Barnacles stud the necklace of my bones.

# THE FAMILY GROUP

That Sunday at the zoo I understood the child
I never had would look like this: stiff-fingered
spastic hands, a steady drool and eyes in cages
with a danger sign. I felt like stone myself
the ancient line curved inward in a sunblind
stare. My eyes were flat. Flat eyes for tanned
young couples with their picture-story kids.

Heads turned our way but you'd learned not to care.
You stood tall as Greek columns, weather-streaked
face bent toward the boy. I wanted to take his hand,
hallucinate a husband. He whimpered at my touch.
You watched me move away and grabbed my other
hand as much in love as pity for our land-
locked town. I heard the visionary rumor of the sea.

What holds the three of us together in my mind
is something no one planned. The chiseled look of mutes.
A window shut to keep out pain. Wooden blank
of doors. That stance the mallet might surprise if it
could strike the words we hoard for fears galloping
at night over moors through convoluted bone.
The strange uncertain rumor of the sea.

# WHEN THE RIVER RISES

The funhouse mirrors swung on tragic hinges:
walls breathing in every enclosed space.
Over my shoulder, Mother's wave threatened
to crush me. I learned to insure against breakage.
Learned to compose my face. Only my head
was covered. She said you couldn't trust
those swindlers at Northwest Mutual Life. Dad
was something else. I cried a lot. Invented
reasons that never told anyone why! The other night
I swear I heard her fake policy expire
in the coal bin. It's happened before. Gilt-framed
photographs burned in the long corridors. I kept
every one, their letters tied in bundles
orderly as blackmail. Father. Mother's son.
The nun that's supposed to be me. Twelve years ago,
my father counted the words he'd buried in a vault
and went to join them. I helped nail down the lid.
Decided to lose the key. Stood over the strapped box
in the family plot and didn't care what the neighbors
said. Last week, still a guest in this
mountainous country, I ate antelope steak
washed down with wine and did not
choke. The image in the Clark Fork of the past spring's
dead buck broke through muddy water
today: drowned body lashed to the monumental
head. I was glad to see the antlers riding towards me.

# ATTACHMENTS

Dead lines. Ice across the continent
breaks the cycle. Beyond repair, Mother's
thick cable with its overload of grim
appliances: clocks and curling irons; a tight
compartment for beating the egg in its shell.
Wherever I walk in winter Father still
moans in my veins. He comes in light on snow,
a gradual thaw.

           The cord lost underwater
towards a green island's lighthouse keeper
freed me of crazed connections. That current
will outlast fortune, massive blackout. But what
about thin nerves, frayed singing from dense
wires? Western Union on my fire escape?
Is code on leased lines a genuine alarm?
And where does the Bitterroot branch
in wrenching snow?

           Perhaps to underground nodes
plumbers whacked looking for a watermain.
Misled by maps they left our neighborhood black
for a week. Cold in a cold season. Wrist-
thick cables that bring New York to my
bedroom phone, the alcove table where breakfast
finds me behind a white screen. An intravenous
transfer pumps juice to my brain.

           This must
be the primitive, pre-chemical shock: electrodes
like an old-fashioned permanent wave
rolled tight against my head in the ultimate

vanity. When they pull the plug I will be somebody
else. Not this plaster woman with a face
of warm snow; breasts rounded towards the hand
withdrawn. Wire bones humming
in relief.

# THE FORGIVENESS

This burlap length could be a shroud, your final
present, Mother. I pulled it from a crowded closet
while your hand stiffened in clutches of rouge and satin,
doctors pronouncing your heart perfect. Threads
of blue and red warm the green turning
from sun. They cross against my skin, light
auburn fires. I am giving you this dahlia bed,
my dive into your darkness, flowers saved
from the long fall, the broken summer. The river
will not hurt us any more. Breathe easy now,
my grounded swimmer, under the butterflies' splash,
weeds swaying, agonized cold currents.

Whatever chokes the stream, hum of alien
traffic, the rock I sit on, rock that weighs me
to the river bottom: everything that moves, loves
and is afraid—we share it all in the still kitchen,
pinned to the floor by our black-eyed bridegroom.
I am wearing your bride sheets for cover, curved
to my body, moulding my deep thighs. I tell you
secrets from my childhood attic, pound the stupid
rag face of Grandmother's doll. I have come
to the last act of the perfect child, dash
this limp form against the splintered floor.

Our tears can run together now. I am not afraid
to let you see them. We call each other across
a narrowing chasm, fear our private line.
I do not have to hide the poems. I am on
my way home to the cat of unexpected leaps, dogs
that bite without warning. Stone lips
will whistle ravishing tunes. Forget about

the ringworm. I would have called if you'd waited
one more day. Wires twisted, I know these rusting
barbs have a spring of their own. I wind it
around this creaking frame dressed in your death
and my bones sing with the long river lapping
the wreck I am, wreck that I may become.

# AN ELEGY FOR GOD
## AND THE WIDOW DAMASCUS

If God is dead He hasn't notified you, Nick Damascus
but sent for your mother instead,
a widow of 67 years, most of them anxious,
waiting for you to walk. She paid, you said,
for your crooked legs. Soon after you came home,
happy from tramping the Peloponnese alone
her thin legs crumpled under and her wide heart
stopped. "Just when she had a little cash to spare,
a few years to enjoy." You shake your fist
at God, who isn't there, and duck off down the street
swinging your cane, wearing that furious limp
with so much style my upright walk's a crippled thing.
Long after, your rhythms sway in my eye and ear,
the Greek fire of your glance, hairy chest,
teeth clenched or parted in bitter laughter,
the embattled stance and that deep look
lashing marble into life. Never in your studio,
in my poems, Nick, I know the restless rush
of your figures: weight and line liberated
from the crutch and leaping in so pure
a dance, I am ashamed to touch your grief
with mine, this slow paralysis.

Alone, I throw myself on the impassioned stone
and kiss the quick hand of your god and mother, dead.

# THE NINTH WAVE

That homer tried for Troy, Montana, put on chains
in Lookout Pass. The drift of heavy drivers
left him fumbling by the roadbed, turned cold
antennae to the higher lows their night
had promised. A trucker skidded towards
the necessary chain of cold events. The day's
misfortune glanced into a headline, dim backshops
of the brain could fold and spindle.

Snow was kinder to the Swan Lake girl thirty feet
from her lonely cabin. It feathered shut
her eyelids on the hillside, floated out the drowning
pet, grounded every vision. Clear ice tolled
crazy wind chimes—last entry in the meditative
journal. No one had foretold this level
in the barometric falling. Counterclockwise winds.
Cold front. Extended outlook: cloudy.

More than music rocked the floor when dancers scattered
in a tidal wave. Years later nothing stands
by the wrecked pavilion. Only wind where naked water ran
echoes in the ear canal. Triskelion limbs tossed outward
from some dark center. Breakers lull the heart valves
ground for disaster. They float us out to set
a channel, lift the chains, our bones light as buoys
letting go of crooked pictures on the shifting wall.

# MOVING IN TIME

## I

Even dead you were a good swimmer. They dragged
the river four days to bring your body in.
By then the waters equalized: so much weight
displaced, leaving you free to float like the car
that drove you, new in the fall, mechanically sane.

That other, older nun, still wearing the long black
deathrobes, strapped in place, current pulsing
through her grim chair. Beyond the pious letters
I am with you, working free of the wreck out there,
my younger friend. They tried to hold you in
with licenses, make her ID yours, no matter.

Behind you someone watched the chassis spin,
your strong hands reassert control. Then
the acrobatic leap past guard rails, learned imperatives.
Your upside-down machine wheeled air.
Five hundred miles east, I hear the tight-wound
four-day watch, prayers less cold and dead,

repeated calls from State Patrols. The old
and sickly shrinking farther back. What is He
trying to tell us? The question, formal, in the only
rhetoric we know. They've buried what you left.
I scream across the party line, mad mourner
in an intermittent wake, waves rocking me down deep.

## II

To find those parts where water laps under pilings:
bones of a dancing girl the beat has forgotten.
Smiling, you riffle the dark for a bright image

till something twists clear and moves on,
free forms over sand. Your breath in a globed float
might resurrect its net. I am learning to follow
slow birds to raucous pickings. The faithful skeleton
lightened. Whitened to stand for itself.

What if I'm half afraid of shifting edges?
The violent river bed in sleep still moving?
Where I drive a road will open—air or water—
past women grieving on the bank. My craft alive
beyond dull cylinders, full as the slow
plum of its own dark drift.

## SELF-SERVICE ISLAND: AN
## ELEGY FROM LANDSEND

This is the jumping off place, scene of the wave rehearsed.
Surface calm trimmed like sails
to the gull's dive, its doubled wingbeat.
These shapes repeated
flow through sleep. Night's drop
over the edge—Aurora Bridge—thin
wash of daybreak.
Fish bubbles here, the rings widening.

Whatever stays down will bloat
as water idles on its tour. Small fins
winnowing the ear.
Rasp of gulls from the crow's-nest.
Near the overpass three lanes backed up
for the exit. Cold to the cross-grained marrow
your bones give back the sun, abstract
themselves around the living.

Who carried the body back from the shore
it leaped for? Salvaged the broadcast parts
anonymous as sand: collarbone
breastbone spleen. Hospital charts.
Deflated lung false
and floating ribs: in that sternal cavity
the heart sustained
its fevers.

Tell me what siren called in murderous traffic.
Whose hand failed your sinking head?
This neck of land, arm of the sea,
treacherous headland

closes. The seawall beaten by the tide, the streaming
turnpike's oblong
concrete wall lapped in the same morning fog
means to divide

fin of car or salmon: chrome
from chrome, chrome
from meat. My automatic noses towards the traffic
island merging
from the street I memorize
that other island. Breathe into the nozzles: gas,
water, air, the odd
long fantasies of nightbirds going home.

# THE PATCHED EYE

looks into its crater, drawn by a quartz gleam
on the rainbarrel. It hears
the bullet sing
light gone away and onyx. The night
clear with a bright half-moon
orbits remembered lashes.
She will have that jewel for her own: the layered
blue and grey of civil war. The dead
weight of his going
turned to a precious stone.

Words from the afternoon come back: failed hand
on the lock, the time
wind made the mountain stand in her way.
The eye is a double-organ driven to converge.
This lover has a foreign tongue.
He speaks through gaps and heavy lids. Waits
in the furnished chamber. The eye
accommodates in pairs: when focus divides
the difference is the same
at one or forty paces.

The wedding book wide on her father's portrait
shows a cutaway vest. The white valentine
of his shirt circles the heart
like a target. All day the daily news
snows against her door. Headlines cloud
with steady pressure. A voice she's heard before
levelled at the phone
goes off in a 20's film: Yes, I am expecting
you for dinner. Ear laid back in the cradle
Why is there so much blood?

## I I

In birds the eye is tubular. In fishes, flat.
Bony plates protect the reptile vision.
A vertical slit in the iris weds some carnivores
to feeble light. Alone,
the woman's eye feeds on itself.
Lobster and prawn do better,
their eyes on stalks articulated
with the head to move in all directions.
Cut off, they sprout
new feelers far from the point of attachment.

X-rays film the foreign object in the skull
near as this day's reminder.
A brainscan picks up damages. They do not tell
what undeveloped prints
inspired this violence, the brain
tired in its pan of bone.
Their work is cold and clinical:
the corneal graft, the glass eye still opaque,
the black patch over the bullet's path
where another bullet waits.

One hundred fifty miles down, these uncut
faces of stone drill towards light.
The odds in gravel and sand, one hundred million
to one. In Kimberley's basic rock, fourteen
million. Miners down on their luck call this
blue ground. Know the curse that follows thieves
and rich owners all the way back to the stolen eye
of an idol. Still they will work sixteen years
for a flash of that blue fire to polarize light,
believing the lode more than hard weight,
steel-blue in a self-inflicted wound. Or the captain's
greed that lowered a slave's dead body like a drowned
cat. They count on crystals fat as a fist
dug out with a penknife more than on carbon they burn
as they tunnel towards black lung.

                                I suppose I could
learn to play oyster, coat minor irritations
with cultured pearls. Forget unbelievable pressures—
a million pounds to the square inch—and heat
too intense to imagine. Except for the unlucky shah
who died under torture refusing to give up the stone
of his father. The Brahman priest in exile. Or the star
of the Folies Bergères done in by a jealous lover.
The diamond brought from Lahore by Queen Victoria.
That Greek broker driven off a windy cliff with his wife
and sons. The mines near Pretoria. Consider Marie
Antoinette moving her jewels aside for the blade
and the gaudy American millionairess smuggled into
the harem to look, who paid by installment—first
money, then a husband gone mad and two children.

Recovery is rare at these levels, the shape of twin
pyramids touching bases more real than a wake.
The lure, the lore of the hidden. Every side
of refractory matter splitting light. A deep
blaze waiting to surface. Bribe, ransom, dowry,
wage. The burning faces near as the constant desert.